curiou$about

HOT RODS

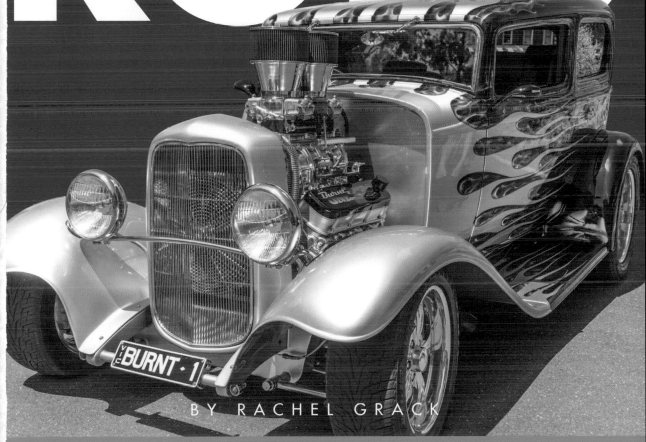

VIC BURNT · 1

BY RACHEL GRACK

AMICUS

What are you

curious about?

CHAPTER THREE

On the Dragstrip
PAGE
16

Curious About is published by
Amicus
P.O. Box 227
Mankato, MN 56002
www.amicuspublishing.us

Editor: Gillia Olson and Alissa Thielges
Designer: Kathleen Petelinsek
Photo researcher: Bridget Prehn

Library of Congress Cataloging-in-Publication Data
Names: Koestler-Grack, Rachel A., 1973- author.
Title: Curious about hot rods / by Rachel Grack.
Description: Mankato, Minnesota : Amicus, 2023. | Series:
Curious about cool rides | Includes bibliographical references
and index. | Audience: Ages 6–9 | Audience: Grades 2–3
Identifiers: LCCN 2020001129 (print)
LCCN 2020001130 (ebook)
ISBN 9781645491156 (library binding)
ISBN 9781681526829 (paperback)
ISBN 9781645491576 (pdf)
Subjects: LCSH: Hot rods—Miscellanea—Juvenile literature.
| Automobiles—Customizing—Miscellanea Juvenile
literature.| Drag racing—Miscellanea—Juvenile literature.
Classification: LCC TL236.3 .K64 2023 (print) | LCC
TL236.3 (ebook) | DDC 629.228/6—dc23
LC record available at https://lccn.loc.gov/2020001129
LC ebook record available at https://lccn.loc.gov/2020001130

Photos © Dreamstime/Matko Medic cover, 1; Shutterstock/
Philip Pilosian 2 (left), 4–5; Shutterstock/Alexander Kondratenko
6–7; Shutterstock/sima 8; Alamy/Andrew Blaida 9; Alamy/
Gary Warnimont 2 (right), 10–11; Alamy/Richard McDowell
12–13; Alamy/Kevin McCarthy 15; Shutterstock/Christopher
Halloran 16–17; Alamy/Jim Monk 18–19; Shutterstock/
DLINE Studios 3, 20; Shutterstock/Praphan Jampala 21

What are hot rods?

Hot rods can be
seen at car shows.

Hot rods are fast cars used for **drag racing**. Some people think only cars made before 1949 can be hot rods. Others say any car can become one. Either way, most start out as normal cars. Then, they get souped up for speed and power.

How do you "soup up" a car?

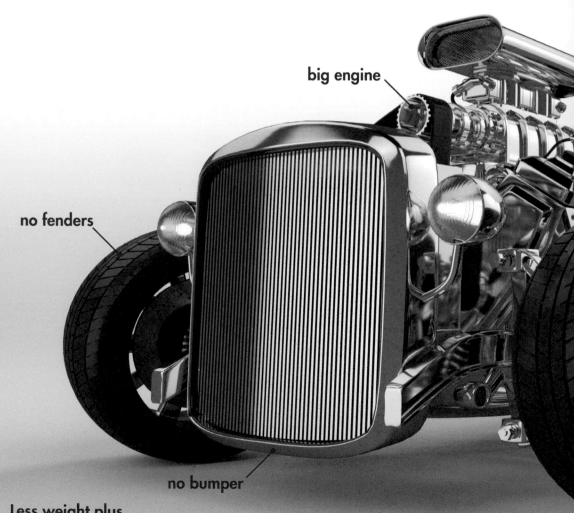

big engine

no fenders

no bumper

Less weight plus
more power means
a faster car.

First, chop the **body**. Take off the roof, hood, windshields, bumpers, and **fenders**. Drop in a bigger engine. Swap in high-power parts. Throw wide tires on the back. Then finish it with a flashy paint job. You're ready to roll!

chopped body

wide tires

camshaft

What's a high-power part?

A part that helps the car perform at its best. Here's an example. All cars have camshafts. These rods control **valves** in the engine. High-power rods let in more air and fuel. This gives a power boost. Some people call them "hot rods." That might be how these cars got named!

High-power parts give hot rods more power.

CHAPTER TWO

What's a common car to use?

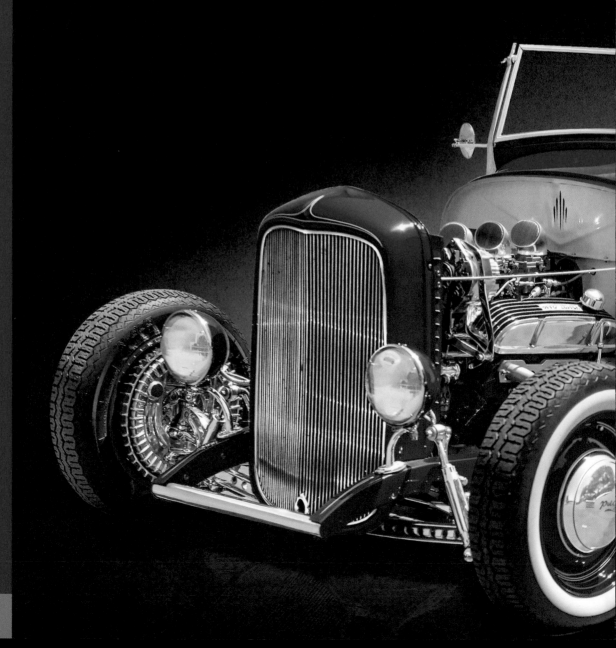

The 1932 Ford roadster is a favorite. Early drivers used them. Their powerful V-8 engines were easy to change. They had lightweight bodies and strong frames. Plus, they looked cool! While the roadster is a classic hot rod, all kinds of cars have been used.

The iconic 1932 Ford roadster is very popular for hot rods.

What fuel do hot rods burn?

DID YOU KNOW?
Regular gas gives hot rods 584 horsepower. Methanol gives them 808 horsepower!

This V8 engine uses nitrous oxide.

Some drivers add **nitrous oxide** (NOS) to the gas. NOS gives more power. Many racers are switching to **methanol**. It produces top power. But there's a downside. Cars burn three times more fuel. That means fewer miles per gallon. Luckily, drag races are short!

Can you drive hot rods on the street?

No. Hot rods are for racing only. **Street rods** are meant for roads, though. They look a lot alike. Street rods are cars made before 1949. They get souped up, too. They're made safe to drive on modern highways.

A 1931 Ford Woodie parked at a car show.

CHAPTER THREE

How fast are hot rods?

A hot rod burns out at the start of a race. This helps it get a good start.

Much faster than regular cars. There are many hot rod **classes**. Engines, fuels, and styles are different in each one. Drag races are usually a quarter mile (0.4 km). The fastest hot rods run a race in 4.4 seconds!

DID YOU KNOW?
A Top Fuel dragster can reach speeds of 330 mph (531 kph)!

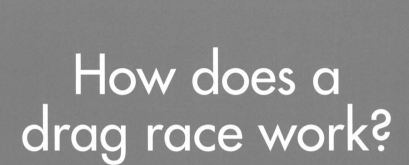

How does a drag race work?

Two hot rods line up to race down a beach.

Usually, two cars line up next to each other. They take off at the same time. The first one to the finish line wins! But that's not always fair. Sometimes, one car gets a head start or starts farther down the track. Then the fastest time wins!

What does it take to be a hot rodder?

A hot rod can reflect a driver's style.

Guts! Drag racing is scary fast. Drivers also need skill. Not just at the wheel, either. Many build their own cars. They know the hot rod inside and out. Do you have a head for cars and a stomach for speed? Let's race!

Hot rodders
should know
how to weld car
parts together.

ASK MORE QUESTIONS

Where can I watch a drag race?

How do people learn to build hot rods?

Try a BIG QUESTION:
What kind of car would you turn into a hot rod?

SEARCH FOR ANSWERS

Search the library catalog or the Internet.
A librarian, teacher, or parent can help you.

Using Keywords
Find the looking glass.

Keywords are the most important words in your question.

?

If you want to:

- watch drag races online, type: DRAG RACE VIDEOS

- learn about building hot rods, type: HOW TO BUILD A HOT ROD

FIND GOOD SOURCES

Here are some good, safe sources you can use in your research.
Your librarian can help you find more.

Books

Hot Rods by Martha London, 2019.

Hot Rods by Thomas Adamson, 2019.

Internet Sites

Motortrend: Hot Rod Network
https://www.motortrend.com/hotrod/
Get the latest news, videos, and more from Hot Rod Network experts. But be aware there may be ads trying to sell things.

The Kids Should See This: Balloon Car Race
https://thekidsshouldseethis.com/post/balloon-car-race-diy-engineering-activity-kids
The Kids Should See This gathers videos appropriate for kids. Be aware there may be a few ads trying to sell things.

Every effort has been made to ensure that these websites are appropriate for children. However, because of the nature of the Internet, it is impossible to guarantee that these sites will remain active indefinitely or that their contents will not be altered.

SHARE AND TAKE ACTION

Hold a pinewood derby car drag race with your friends.
Make a dragstrip on your driveway or front sidewalk. Take turns, and see who wins!

Build a hot rod model!
Purchase a hot rod model kit from a local store. You could try a V-8 engine model, too. Ask an adult to help you put it together.

Design your own hot rod.
Many hot rods have artistic paint jobs. Design a paint job all your own!

GLOSSARY

body The outer shell of a car.

class A group of cars defined by certain features, such as size, body shape, and modifications.

drag racing Races—usually a quarter-mile (0.4 km) long— between two vehicles.

dragstrip The strip of road used for a drag race.

fender A part around the wheel of a car.

methanol A liquid fuel made from methane and used in race cars.

nitrous oxide A gas of nitrogen and oxygen that can increase engine power.

street rod A type of hot rod that can be driven on regular streets; some race and some do not.

valve A part that can stop or start the flow of air or liquid.

INDEX

About the Author

Rachel Grack has been editing and writing children's books since 1999. She lives on a ranch in Arizona. Hot cars have always fired her up! At one time, she even owned a street rod—a 1965 Ford Galaxie 500. She loved cruising with the windows down. This series refueled her passion for cool rides!